Calm in the Chaos:

Discover techniques that will empower you to
break free from stress

Calm in the Chaos:

Discover techniques that will empower you to break free from stress

Kristine Iverson

Calm in Chaos
Copyright © 2021 Kristine Iverson

Printed in the United States of America

Kristine Iverson
1603 Capitol Ave, Suite 310 A552,
Cheyenne WY 82001

ISBN: 978-0-578-98756-9

Contents

Chapter 3:

Chapter 4

Legal Disclaimer

This book has been written and published strictly for information; purposes, and in no way should it be used as a substitute for consultation wit a healthcare professional. You should not consider educational material herei to be the practice of medicine or to replace consultation with a physicia or other medical practitioner. The author and publisher are providing yo with information so that you can choose, at your own risk, to act on th; information. The author and publisher urge all readers to be aware of the health status and to consult health professionals before beginning any healt program.

Acknowledgments

This is my first journey in writing and publishing a book. A huge THANK YOU to friends who have offered support, encouragement, and advice. Thank you to Shelley Heffer, David Alecock, Alexa Stone, Angi Bellingar, Jill Hamilton, Kris Kemp, Mandi Graziano, Danielle Kessinger, and Yvette Sechrist McGlasson.

Dedication

This book is dedicated to Jennifer Kay Iverson.

You were a portal to another world. A beautiful, brilliant light that shone brighter than the stars. I love you, and will always admire your unique, fierce spirit. I stood in awe at your strength as we navigated our homelife together. I often feel as though I do not honor your memory enough. I dedicate this book to you, your beauty, bold heartedness, and supportive strength from the beyond. Thank you for your support and guidance in being my big sis.

Jennifer Kay Iverson - 1976 to 1990

Jennifer Kay Iverson, at the age of 13, was hit by a car and passed away unexpectedly. Her life and passing changed me and our family forever.

Introduction

The journey of writing my first book was a process of making a commitment, putting the project down, picking it back up, and questioning if I was going to complete this. I used time blocks and time management tools and also had compassion for myself and an understanding that life will get in the way. This was a self-motivation project, where I knew I had to push myself to complete it. In moments of overwhelm or confusion, I successfully pulled on some of the exercises that I am sharing here.

This book, in part, is a final healing process of a mental health journey that I am now choosing to share publicly. *Calm in the Chaos* is not a self-help book focused on "pampering" or a spa visit to make you feel good for an hour. *Calm in the Chaos* is a tool to help you succeed and grow in nearly any area of life.

Chapter 1

Path to Well-Being

I remember sitting on my dorm room floor in the early 2000s, contemplating my life after graduation. Frankly, I wasn't sure what I should do. Yes, I had my degree . . . Like most of my peers, I was wondering what success looked like? What was the best way to go? And most importantly at the time, what did I want to do for a living?

The one thing crystal clear to me was that I was nourished by travel. It was a passion and one that I decided I wanted to pursue for the rest of my life. Travel made me feel alive. When I stepped into another country or new surroundings, I instantly felt a surge of energy.

I first discovered this passion my sophomore year in college when I was accepted for a semester in London with my philosophy professor and about 15 other students. It was my first time out of the country and I was able to study philosophy and religion in an area so rich in history. I'm the type of person who enjoys pondering questions like, "Are humans obligated to better themselves, and will that make them happier? What is happiness? If everyone spoke their mind would the world be a better place? Does utilizing time properly make our lives meaningful and happy?"

I was so excited on this trip to be planning a visit to Germany for Oktoberfest. I remember the shot of adrenaline I felt at the Eiffel Tower on a weekend get-away and walking down Abbey Road in London to replicate the Beatles' classic album cover. I wanted to tap into that energy, excitement, and passion—nothing compared to this travel high!

I was aware that this was a privilege. My mother sacrificed more than I will say so I could go to college. I deeply appreciated from a place of gratitude the opportunity to meet other cultures, and experience life this way.

Despite this privilege, all was not perfect and I felt the standard pressures of college life, the drive to succeed. And I hadn't learned yet how to set health boundaries for myself.

Setting Boundaries

My semester abroad turned out far more than I expected it to be. N matter what country I visited, I found a small part of me that belonged ther The experience was mind-blowing.

"A true community is not just about being geographically close to someone or part of the same social web network. It's about feeling connected and responsible for what happens. Humanity is our ultimate community, and everyone plays a crucial role." - Yehuda Berg

Naturally, after that astonishing semester abroad of visiting many countrie and having amazing philosophical discussions in a flat in London, I believe my best path was to do something where I could build a career, not just trave as a casual tourist. Travel made me come alive and it also allowed time an space to ponder the philosophical questions I enjoyed spending time thinkin about. "Does living your life for others make your life have meaning? Doe life have a reason? Is death a new beginning? What is human consciousness?

Cruise ships were my answer. I had never taken a cruise, yet I knew th sailing the high seas was my next step. Applying online wasn't getting m anywhere. It took months to find the right person. I was able to obtain a direc line to the Entertainment Department's shoreside hiring manager. Once I di I left messages, sent reminder emails, and let him know that I was just goin to be in the area (5 hours from home!) this week. Would he have some time t meet? It worked! By obtaining this dream job, I had proof, that when I kno what I want, I will be relentless in the pursuit of it.

Cruise life fueled my passion for human connectivity and adventure. Ad in getting paid for it and this whole idea was music to my ears. I romanticized the ships, as many newcomers do. One time on the dance floor, a guest said to me, "I wish I would have done this! Before I had kids, my house, job, I always wanted to do this!" I remember being overwhelmed with gratitude for the opportunity I had been given.

Cruise life had a downside too. I was engulfed in a profession that was a lifestyle, a global subculture, which guests, even friends, and family, could not understand. As a guest, the cruise is glamorous, every meal is catered, and entertainment is brought to you. The staff, on the other hand, works long hours, seven days a week. We literally ran from activity to activity. The biggest challenge was to maintain the euphoric energy level that was expected of us, 24/7, during the entire cruise.

I soon realized that I must find a way to balance my strong work ethic and the need to maintain that momentum for days on end. After all, the magic of cruises is letting passengers feel that we all equally enjoy the experience.

Most Americans who join ships are usually in the Entertainment Department. Frequently as singers or dancers. I started as cruise staff, the activities fun person. Later in life, I would return as an Assistant Cruise Director and a Training Officer with other cruise lines.

The staff has rules and pressures that do not exist for guests. We work long hours every single day. Depending on your position on board, a typical contract would last six months. Still, it can be nine months for many crew positions or four months for higher positions onboard. With NO days off. After the contract ends, one gets 9–12 weeks off, unpaid. Contract length and time off lengths vary based on position. It can feel like you are on-call 24/7 while on board. When something goes wrong, they can call you at nearly any time to help fix it

Part of the challenge of cruise ship life for a guest-facing position is that you are never truly off. You are always "in the office." When you are in port, you run into guests and other crew members. Even when you are not with the cruise guests, you are still with your co-workers, supervisor, and management. When I was off the ship. I was excited to have as many experiences as I possibly could. The thought of staying on board and taking a nap, instead of going out in port, never occurred to me.

Of course, it's not all negative. Depending on your position and the country you are from, the salary can be great and the crew becomes like family. The sense of camaraderie among the crew is incomparable to anything on land. Overall, the experience can be very rewarding.

On my first contract, I did not have proper self-care routines established. I was mesmerized by the newness and adjusting to an entirely new lifestyle. I recall how the days of the week no longer had relevance. Days were referred to as embark day, sea day, port day, sea day, disembark, etc. I was not in tune with what was happening internally; only in reflection could I see that I was losing my grounding.

"My drive for work literally drove me crazy. I had a mental breakdown on the ship. I lost my speaking voice on the boat and was disembarked."

My drive for work literally drove me crazy. I had a mental breakdown on the ship. I lost my speaking voice on the boat and was disembarked. An ambulance showed up and took me to the hospital. I remained tied to a bed for days in a delusional state.

I stayed in a hospital in Portugal where I jumped out of a second-story window, ran to the beach, and went for a swim in the ocean. How could I deal with my own self-sabotage? Why did this happen? The doctor that treated me told my family he was deeply concerned for me. Eventually, a nurse tranquilizers in hand, escorted me on a flight home, where I was hospitalized.

I walked away from this traumatic experience stunned. Would I lose my job? What would my family say? Was I going to be okay?

My mom is my greatest treasure. She supports me 100%, however, she was not equipped to deal with this, through no fault of her own. I was sinking in disappointment. I felt empty and unable to get out of that hole while going through this dark chapter. Once I got back home, I was able to begin therapy and began my journey towards self-care and self-acceptance.

According to the World Health Organization, every 40 seconds, a person commits suicide, mainly between 15-29 years of age (World Health Organization, "Suicide," 2019). A large contributing factor to this may be due to the pressure imposed by society with unhealthy lifestyles. Things have not improved. In fact, when the National Institute of Mental Health (NIMH) broke down the report by ethnicity, age, and gender, the results were shocking, highlighting a considerable gap, especially among 18- to 25-year-olds.

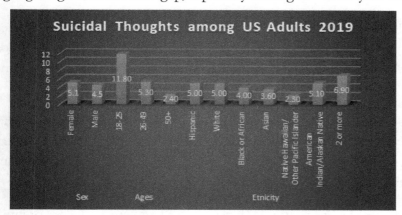

Only in retrospect can I look back 20 years and see clearly that many of my decisions after working on cruise ships were directly related to this experience. In therapy, a question came up and changed everything: What am I doing to help myself? I had given all my trust to outsiders, but I had no faith in myself.

The fear of failure muted my inner voice. I was stuck on the ridiculous idea of "everything will be ok without doing anything." This simplistic strategy avoids the fundamental and essential obligation we all have: well-being with ourselves.

How to Start?

It took me years to heal, and longer still to share my experience. Now tha I have, my intention is to make it easier for someone else. The first step for m was to set boundaries.

Boundaries are based on our perceptions and our past experiences Boundaries can have many forms and vary from person to person. Al-Anoi uses two well-known sayings to set healthy boundaries: "live and let live'" anc "quit taking it personally."

People are going to do whatever they are going to do, regardless of wha I think or believe. I simply need to allow for them to be themselves. Wha happens on a daily basis, what people say or how they react actually has nothing to do with me. It is critical to remember this when I begin to react.

What do healthy boundaries look like? Boundaries are guidelines or limit that you set for your own self-care and then communicate to others so the know where your limits are. It helps others to know how to interact with you and what will happen if your boundaries are crossed.

Types of Boundaries

There are many types of boundaries set for a variety of needs and reason and can apply to family, co-workers, partners, dating relationships, children, o friends:

1. Physical needs (i.e., need for personal space)
2. Time
3. Conversations
4. Sexual
5. Financial
6. Personal needs

When I was younger, I was the type of person who would do anything or anyone, to my own detriment. I wouldn't take into account the level of friendship I had with the person asking. I would overextend myself even for a mild acquaintance. If someone called for a pick-up on the other side of town at 11 pm, I would jump in my car and race to the rescue. If someone asked me to help them move on a Saturday, okay. From errands to a listening ear until 2 am, I wanted to be there for anyone and everyone.

I still have the same heart to help others; however, I have learned to *set boundaries*. In the past, I suffered from emotional and physical fatigue from over-extending myself. Setting healthy boundaries allowed me to identify my own needs as well as distance myself from those who took advantage of my willingness to help.

Now when I'm asked to do a favor or make plans, I practice stepping back to assess the larger picture. What is being asked? What do I have on my plate in terms of other commitments? What is my energy level? Is this something I would enjoy or does it feel heavy? This is still a practice for me, I find myself being successful in moments and other times still overextending myself. Remember, it's a practice.

How Do You Set Healthy Boundaries?

Three reminders for setting healthy boundaries:

1. **Communicate your limitations** – Tell employers, friends, and family when you are available and for what. This creates a clear strucure and freedom to work inside some clearly set boundaries.

2. **Take time for yourself** – In times of high stress, I have a whit-board hanging on my wall. I list about 20 self-care practices, such as nature walk, calling someone, getting a massage, read-write-breath stop, create an adventure. Then in a moment of need, I can glance at the board and see clear options to choose from.

3. **Learn to let go** – Holding on to a negative comment someone else said or a small mistake is not going to serve you in any way.

"In a nutshell, it's knowing how to separate your feelings or 'stuff' from someone else's," says U.K.-based psychologist Dr. Tara Quinn-Cirillo. "As human beings, we have our own thoughts, memories, and lived experiences and sometimes that can become very blurred with someone else's. Boundaries are healthy for helping you identify and keep that space."

Setting boundaries is beneficial for far more than just defining our identity. Having them in place can limit your stress level and the body's production of stress hormones such as cortisol and adrenaline. Creating and keeping boundaries will ultimately protect our mental well-being.

Why Set Boundaries?

We set boundaries for a reason. Usually, it is for a healthy relationship with self or another. Boundaries allow us to set clear expectations and avoid feelings of anger, disappointment, or resentment.

Here are six qualities that assist in creating healthy boundaries:

1. Be positive: Boundaries should be both supportive of you and of other people in a healthy, positive way. *Our primary commitment is to our own self-care.*

2. Belong: The need to belong is natural. This is why we create societies and communities. Belonging to something greater than yourself is essential.

3. Based on your strengths: While you should always be open to learning and growing, you intrinsically have some stronger skill sets. Instead of engaging in a constant fight to overcome your weaknesses, a wiser approach is to become a specialist in an area that is your strong suit. For example, I know I do not have a mechanical mind so I would not spend years trying to become an architect, for example. But I do have a creative mind and so have been successful in thinking outside the box.

This focus is one of the secrets of successful people. They focused on their skills and became specialists; as a result, they achieved something meaningful.

4. Focused on self-care: Boundaries establish expectations. They allow ou to state expectations to another and establish what others can expect from ou. Being able to set healthy boundaries can be empowering.

5. Respect other's boundaries: Respect for other people is essential. omeone's boundaries tell us how they want to be treated. We don't want to lisrespect other's boundaries; they have those boundaries for a reason and we ave to respect those limits to have a healthy relationship.

6. Be followed regardless of emotion: Boundaries need to be defined nd adhered to regardless of emotion. For example, if you are a parent and our child wants to spend ten hours a day on video games, you as an adult now it's best for them to not have ten hours of screen time. Even if your hild throws a temper tantrum, stick to the boundaries that you clearly explain o your child.

Others' Boundaries

What happens when I am not aware of another's boundaries? What can do when they are not expressed or set?

Instead of assuming, ask. If you think that someone is uncomfortable with omething, check-in with them. Ask direct, clear questions. Ask, "what is your preference?"

Recognize what is yours. What are your problems to solve and take esponsibility for? What are the other person's problems for them to solve? f someone does not communicate their boundaries, you can communicate ours.

Learn to Say "No"

It is critical in setting healthy boundaries that we learn to say "no." Saying no protects our personal space, our headspace, and our time. The reasons we might not speak up can vary. It could be because we fear being rejected or being left out. We may feel uncomfortable or embarrassed and we don't want o say no because we think it's the wrong thing. Being overly concerned with vhat someone thinks of us can make us feel anxious or worried.

In short, we place our well-being in another's hand, in assumptions, and ultimately, we mute our inner voice to give priority to others. Subconsciously our mind may believe that our opinion is worthless.

Learning to say no is a job that takes practice, especially when we are interacting with our parents, partner, and other loved ones. We may be aware that our loved one loves us unconditionally; however, it is important they respect our boundaries. Practice saying "no" when necessary. I am still practicing and love it when I get opportunities to practice saying, "thank you, no."

Certainly, they may not always agree because everyone has their own opinion, but it is necessary for our mental and emotional health for those close to us to respect us when we say no.

"Practice saying 'no' when necessary. I am still practicing and love it when I get opportunities to practice saying, 'thank you, no.'"

A few examples of how to gracefully say "no."

Offer an alternative. I am not going to be able to fulfill this request however, I can offer you . . . instead. For example, I could say: I can't take you to the store right now but I can take you in five hours.

1. This request is outside of my area of expertise and I don't feel I would be the best or strongest person for the job. If I can make a referral to someone else I will.

2. If a request is too large, think of a smaller way to assist. I may not be able to head up the entire committee, however, I can assist by being a part of the committee.

3. Looks like a great time, thank you for inviting me, however, I have another commitment. I'll look for the pictures on Facebook.

The Positive Side of Stress – Eustress

Did you know that there is a positive side to stress? It's what fuels our successes and achievements. It is called eustress and you may be experiencing it if you feel eager, excited, thrilled, proud, resilient, determined, fulfilled, or in a state of flow. Distressing and tough circumstances can lead us to experience healthy eustress—as we learn to cope and develop greater strength, determination, and courage.

Usually, it is *distress* that comes to mind for many of us when we think of stress. We use the word stress to mean distress. The prefrontal cortex of our brain is most susceptible to stress. It is where our executive functioning lies. Even with mild amounts of stress, our ability to think and process is inhibited. We automatically shift to our primal state of fight or flight.

We often hear statements like "I want to live a quiet, stress-free life," or "this job doesn't work because it causes me stress," perhaps even the phrase "my (insert person's name here) stresses me out, I can't live like this" sneaks out of your mouth. We tend to look at the term "stress" in a pejorative way. It is a kind of fictional "enemy" that we have created. However, like pretty much everything in life, stress has nuances; it can be as beneficial as it can be detrimental, which is why the same stimulus can be called "stress" or "eustress," depending on how we use it.

I'm more of an extrovert, I experience my eustress easily at a social event. Take the same event and for an introvert, the social situation throws them into distress. In the short term, eustress provides us with an energy boost to perform challenging activities like playing a competitive sport or public speaking. In the longer term, eustress helps us keep working at things, especially when the going gets tough, e.g., learning and growing as we move on with our lives after a rejection or continuing to study when we'd really rather give up!

The Other Side – Distress

The World Health Organization defines stress as "the set of physiological reactions that prepare the body for action" (International Labour Organization and WHO Committee on Occupational Health. Psychosocial Factors at Work: Recognition and Control. Occupational Safety and Health Series No. 56, 1984).

Some of the first research on stress was in the 1930s. Hans Selye, endocrinologist, Doctor of Medicine and Chemistry, recognized a behavioral pattern that he originally called "general adaptation syndrome." In short, it is a biological warning system necessary for survival.

I have already mentioned that our prefrontal cortex is our most evolved brain region that holds our highest order of cognitive abilities. The hippocampus region of our brain specializes in processing sets of stimuli, in other words, the context of a situation. For example, if one had a traumatic experience with a cat when a child, now as an adult when they see a cat, their palms sweat or their heart rate rises. It is because of the hippocampus region of our brain and its close connections with the amygdala that the entire context associated with a traumatic event can provoke anxiety.

The amygdala is where many sensory inputs converge to inform us of potential dangers in our environment. Called by many our reptilian brain, we get sent into fight or flight coming from this most basic place.

"While we have been studying stress for more than 100 years, the stigmas surrounding it still persist."

While we have been studying stress for more than 100 years, the stigmas surrounding it still persist. Stress will always exist, especially when facing a challenge, a change, or an adverse action. It is a natural response of the body.

Path to Happiness

One could view life as a path that goes up and down, filled with people and experiences that follow life's decisions. The same thing can be said of happiness—it is not a destination, it is a path.

In childhood, we were curious explorers, looking forward to discovering the world. Everything seemed new and wonderful. We admired even the palms of our hands, mom's smile, dad's games, snowflakes; in short, we appreciate our surroundings and are grateful. We come into the world as a clean slate, open and in the receiving mode.

Later, we experience relentless pressures in daily life. It is imperative to strengthen our emotional health. When we do this, our perspective changes. It is not about being happy every day or that you will never face adversities, it is about meeting life with a positive attitude.

Martin Seligman, Ph.D., who was president of the American Psychological Association (APA) for more than a decade, made a profound study of the meaning of life through his patients. The triggers of depression, feeling stuck, and even death were crucial topics in his study. Dr. Seligman and his peers then developed a formula to summarize the pursuit of true happiness, PERMA:

Positive Emotion

Engagement

Relationships

Meaning

Achievement

Positive Emotions: One of the foundations of well-being. Human beings are emotional, and like everything else in life, the spectrum of these feelings ranges from j.oy, happiness, and love to anger, sadness, and grief.

On the way to well-being, it's vital to vibrate with positive emotions, such as kindness, gratitude, hope, fulfillment, belief, and even optimism. All of them boost personal well-being. However, this doesn't mean that the rest of the emotions disappear or should be ignored. Instead, they should be acknowledged, but we must find a mechanism for the positive to overcome them.

Engagement: Being totally absorbed ("in the flow") by an activity when time and self-consciousness seem to cease. Dr. Mihály Csíkszentmihályi, specialist in the field, explains the subject as the satisfying power of how to achieve total immersion in your daily life. When we are engaged in a eustress activity, we find ourselves in the flow. For an extrovert, it is a party, for a herbalist, it's gardening, for an athlete it's running a marathon. We become so engaged, we lose track of time.

Relationships: We are "social beings," whether we like it or not, we are co-dependent. Therefore, keeping healthy relationships is an important part of well-being. It is worth emphasizing that the first healthy relationship we should have is with ourselves. People who have strong positive relationships are generally happier in life.

Meaning: True happiness can come from creating and having meaning in life; having a purpose larger than yourself. Serving something more significant than one's self is one way that people find purpose in life.

Achievement: As Heraclitus said, "change is the only constant," and those constant changes are oriented towards new improvements, goals, or fulfillment. Even in our less pleasant facets, there is an internal purpose. Having goals and meeting them is indeed one of the pillars of our life. Choosing the right path vibrates with positive emotions, so you will improve your well-being and allow yourself to flourish.

PERMA Quiz

Below you will find a survey that you are asked to rate on a scale of to 10. Please circle the frequency that best describes your answer. At the end count the total scores. It will take you about five minutes.

I kindly ask you to be honest in doing so; even if you must take a few extra minutes to think about it, remember that your well-being is an inner and personal endeavor well worth being addressed.

Always   **Never**

	10	9	8	7	6	5	4	3	2	1
How satisfied are you with your personal relationships?	10	9	8	7	6	5	4	3	2	1
How much of the time do you feel close to accomplishing your main goal?	10	9	8	7	6	5	4	3	2	1
How often do you lose track of time while working?	10	9	8	7	6	5	4	3	2	1
In general, how often do you feel loved?	10	9	8	7	6	5	4	3	2	1
Would you say that most of your activities bring you anxiety?	10	9	8	7	6	5	4	3	2	1
How often do you lose track of time while you are at home?	10	9	8	7	6	5	4	3	2	1
How often do you joyfully go about your daily activities?	10	9	8	7	6	5	4	3	2	1
How lonely do you feel?	10	9	8	7	6	5	4	3	2	1

How often do you handle and solve your responsibilities? 10	9	8	7	6	5	4	3	2	1
With the concept of meaning in mind, how often do you think your life is meaningful? 10	9	8	7	6	5	4	3	2	1
How often do you feel angry in your daily life? 10	9	8	7	6	5	4	3	2	1
In general, how often do you receive support from others? 10	9	8	7	6	5	4	3	2	1
How often would you describe your life as satisfying? 10	9	8	7	6	5	4	3	2	1
In general, how often do you bring support to others? 10	9	8	7	6	5	4	3	2	1
How often do you think about reaching your goals? 10	9	8	7	6	5	4	3	2	1
How often are you grateful? 10	9	8	7	6	5	4	3	2	1
If someone asked you about your positive emotional connection, you 10	9	8	7	6	5	4	3	2	1

would say it is...										
How often do you wonder if you might change your current situation?	10	9	8	7	6	5	4	3	2	1
How happy would you say you are?	10	9	8	7	6	5	4	3	2	1
How often do you take steps that bring closeness to your well-being?	10	9	8	7	6	5	4	3	2	1
TOTAL										

Add up your individual scores and divide by 10 to get your PERMA number.

180-200 points. Your PERMA is 9 to 10 points. This is the highest score on the scale. Your well-being is the most important to you, and you regularly celebrate it. Kudos to you. It's your job to keep it that way. Reinforcing the knowledge you have will help you stay on track, and in the following chapters, you will find some tools to help you.

160-179 points. Your PERMA is 8 to 8.99 points. You are very close to reaching the peak of your well-being. Your actions are well on track, one more step and you are almost there. In the following chapters, you will find some tips and suggestions to help you take further action towards your goal.

140-159 points. Your PERMA is 7 to 7.99 points. This is the most common range, according to experts. Personal growth is knocking at your door. I kindly invite you to open your doors to move forward.

120-139 points. Your PERMA is 6 to 6.99. You are probably more oriented towards "Doing" or "Having" as a sense of happiness. The invitation is to move closer to "Being," a space where all factors combine and balance forces to achieve the greater good. Keep moving forward.

110-119 points. Your PERMA is 5.5 to 5.99 points. There is a wake-up call in your results, and you may need more support.

In the following pages you will find valuable information that will help guide you to "calm in the chaos" on your well-being journey.

If you are looking for more information, please visit the website https://permahsurvey.com/.

Notes:

Chapter 2

Transition into a Balanced Life

After my breakdown, I started to explore mind-body wellness and healing modalities. I took a year off for exploration. I read books, attended therapy, went on many nature walks, and journaled. The element of shame inhibited my recovery process because the natural human state is to spring forward and be resilient.

I became a huge proponent of self-care and an advocate for healing. There were a few select friends that I spoke with about my experience. For the most part, I felt a lot of embarrassment and shame about the breakdown. This was a typical response because our society did not discuss mental health all that openly at the time. Now social media encourages people to share their experiences.

We have more resources today than ever before. TV series such as *Heal*, *Rotten*, *Boy Interrupted*, *13 Reasons Why*, *Maniac*, even *Robin Williams: Come Inside My Mind*, showcase how we need to speak up and support each other to solve this public health issue.

Marni Stahlman, president and CEO of the Mental Health Association of Central Florida says: "As human beings, we should make an attempt to give ourselves permission to be happy. To explore creative outlets that can reduce our stressors. Grant ourselves permission that some days we may not be happy. It is equally okay to have a sad day. Give yourself permission and forgiveness to be sad. It is okay to reach out for help. Understand where your shame comes from on those unhappy days. Don't isolate, push past the shame. Find that one person who can help you through. So it does not become debilitating or chronic. Have a commitment to both the happy days and unhappy days.

I get asked all the time: What's the most important thing that can promote good mental health? I respond, find your laugh. It's really that simple. Find your release, your joy, and laugh."

A popular break that my company, CROW Practice, offers our meeting clients when it is a meeting marathon, has been our 15-minute laughter session. The age-old saying that laughter is the best medicine has a lot of truth to it. It lowers our stress hormones and our blood pressure. Laughter can increase our oxygen intake and impact our immune system. It can lift our spirits as well as provide a bit of a cardio workout similar to burning the same amount of calories as a brisk walk.

The interesting thing about laughter is we can experience all of the same benefits when we are fake laughing. Our laughter does not even have to be genuine to experience these great benefits. Our bodies cannot distinguish the difference between true laughter and faking it. The ground rules for a laughter session are to be playful and don't take yourself seriously. Even though we may have the proper tools, we often don't use them. Many tend to focus on "survive" rather than "live."

A balanced life is a constant work in progress. It is not a goal to be achieved, it's a continuous awareness in situations, intentionally choosing the best for ourselves. For example, we've all heard that we cannot give from an empty cup or that we should put our oxygen mask on first on an airplane before assisting others.

One of my favorite Elizabeth Gilbert quotes in *Eat Pray Love* is: "People tend to think that happiness is a stroke of luck, something that will descend like fine weather if you're fortunate. But happiness is the result of effort. You fight for it, strive for it, insist upon it, and sometimes even travel around the world looking for it. You have to participate relentlessly".

What is Stopping You?

What keeps us from achieving our dreams or goals? One reason is clarity. Oftentimes we are not clear with exactly what we want. We simply thought the dream or goal would just come to us. For example, if you want to buy a house, you have steps: protecting your credit rating, saving for the down payment, and selecting a realtor, to name a few steps.

There is a lot of research that advocates writing down your goals and re-evaluating them from time-to-time in order to achieve those goals. Writing helps us gain clarity.

Traditionally, there are many reasons that keep us from reaching our goals but the three that have affected me the most are fear, time, and my own limiting beliefs.

Fear of failing, of being wrong, of disappointing others, and ultimately of failure. Society often tells us that failure is the second-worst thing that could happen to us (the first is death). If we were to envision failure it would be a hideous monster. However, every achievement is the result of failures. For example, Dr. Seuss dropped out of college and his first book was rejected by publishers 28 times. But by the time of his death he had sold over 600 million copies of his books.

Time is our greatest equalizer. No one has more time in the day than others. It is truly the only limited resource we have. While we can earn more money, we can not earn more time.

Limiting beliefs can look and sound like many different things. For example, I'm not good enough. Which is absurd. People are made of their experiences and learning. What makes you think that your experiences are less valuable than others?

Limiting Beliefs

Limiting beliefs are false beliefs that prevent us from pursuing our goal or desires. Our beliefs put boundaries and limitations on what we perceive to be reasonable behavior. Some limiting beliefs can be helpful, for example believing that stealing is wrong.

The question becomes, where do our limiting beliefs come from? In the beginning, when we were children, the world was a wonderful place. Everything was fascinating as we learned to walk, talk, taste, smell, hear, touch, and feel. We loved and accepted our bodies. We stared at ourselves in the mirror. But somewhere along the way, we began to mimic our parents, taking on their likes and dislikes, creating what we perceived to be our own preferences. However, the strong influences of family, teachers, neighbors, friends . . . eventually we began to believe every word that someone else said about us and to us. And that is the voice that today, as adults, we listen to constantly.

You know the one . . . it tells you that you are too tall, too short, too old, too young; it's the one that tells you that you are not good enough. It is this false and limiting belief system that is the foundation of every limiting belief that you have today.

3 Types of Limiting Beliefs

1. *Limiting beliefs about yourself* – When or if you feel you cannot do something because something is wrong with you or you think: "I'm not good enough."

2. *Limiting beliefs about the world* – When you feel you are unable to do something because of another or the constructs of society, the world rules, laws.

3. *Limiting beliefs about life* - When you feel like you can't do something because it's too difficult.

"Whether you think you can, or you think you can't—you're right." - Henry Ford

Example of Limiting Beliefs - We All Have Them

The pastor of a Unity Church shared a story about the escape artist Harry Houdini. Houdini said that he would get out of any jail cell and had been successful up until this point. He was struggling with this particular lock, it seemed different, he was unable to figure it out. Exhausted and with a feeling of defeat he collapsed with his back against the door and the door swung open! The entire time this door was never locked. This is a great example of how we lock ourselves up in limiting beliefs, when in reality the door is not even locked!

How Do We Overcome Our Limiting Beliefs?

1. Ask yourself, "What If I'm Wrong?" Generally, limiting beliefs lose their power as soon as we consider that they may not be true.

The belief that financial security comes from having a good job and a steady paycheck. This is a belief that many people believe, and there is truth to it. Entrepreneurs would disagree or at least also add that financial security can be achieved by other means. Allowing money to work for me, investments, etc.

2. Ask Yourself, "How Is This Belief Serving Me?"

I've had the belief that I'm better off alone for most of my life. I don't need or want a partner. It's served me well in the sense that I am comfortable in my own skin and enjoy my own company. I have questioned recently if I'm missing out by not having a partner.

3. Create Alternative Beliefs

One time I was traveling in Ecuador and I was intending to start a new full-time job when I returned home. After months of job hunting, I had signed the offer paperwork and was expecting to take my trip to Ecuador and return home to my new full-time job. I received an email that my direct supervisor was leaving so they had eliminated my new position. I was devastated, however, I chose to create the belief that I was meant to spend more time in Ecua dor. That is exactly what I did. I ended up spending two months longer on m travel adventure. Living on a farm with Hari Krishna's, making communial meals, and bringing travels back to the farm.

Belief System

To transform your belief systems, use an intention or affirmation tha simply states "I am (insert your word of preference like strong, loving, kind intelligent)." Avoid using the "I will be (X)" as this indicates that you will b this sometime in the future. Creating new belief systems is simply returning t your natural state of being. Every time you find yourself in some self-defeatin inner dialogue, stop and say out loud "cancel cancel" and then follow it wit your new intention. I AM AMAZING.

1. Once you have created your new intention, use it everywhere. Plac post-it notes around your house in the most unexpected location Stand in the bathroom and gaze deeply into your eyes as you brus your teeth . . . reflecting on and repeating the new intention silently

2. Carry the intention with you into your meditation practice. Recor yourself saying the intention over and over again for 20-30 minute and listen to it every time you work out.

3. Let go of the "shoulda, coulda, woulda" language. Instead of sayin to yourself, "I should be a better mom/partner/friend," pivot you dialog into "I am a good mom/partner/friend." What happens ove time is that the inner critic begins to quiet and your mind begir to accept your intention as your new reality and YOU have made major paradigm shift.

Protect Your Temple

As the old saying goes, your body is a temple. Protecting it is a must. Striving to be physically fit is of little use if our emotions are unbalanced and vice versa. Focusing on only one of these core areas is unhealthy because we are an interactive machine. Every part of us is connected and dependent on whole chain of processes. So, when I talk about protection, I mean to align thought with action to get closer to a mind-body balance.

Dr. Michelle Trias defines balance and healing for us: "To have authentic healing, you must look at the body holistically. The definition of holistic is relating to the complete systems, rather than the parts to treat mind and body." She adds an invitation to deepen our holistic vision as women by saying: "As women, we are over-committed, overworked, overtired and so many of us are suffering with chronic illnesses with no end in sight. Just endless trips to the pharmacy month after month and year after year. Step One in anyone's wellness journey is to make a commitment to your health. They don't call it a healthy journey because it's fast and easy. There is also so much information out there about one diet or another that it is hard to know what to believe. I like to keep it VERY simple. Here is the secret: eat more foods that are alive, growing towards the sun, and eat fewer foods that are frozen, processed, junk, and dead. Sounds simple because it really is. When you get your energy from food, your body and brain work at their best and real healing is possible."

In the following pages, we will learn about tools to use on our "Path to Well-being." I am providing some tools here in the following pages developed from my 20 years of experience that have helped me and I hope some of them work for you. If one person takes away one tool, then this book was a success for me.

Take Action

Move Out of Your Comfort Zone

In an interview with Saima Bhatti, LAc, DOM, owner of Awaken Integrative Health Centers, she said, "As human beings, we make decisions in our lives. Then we confine our view of life based on those decisions we made. We take those experiences forward, allowing them to act as our life lessons determining how we see ourselves and the rest of the world. Learning and growing from our early years can reveal how we have constrained ourselves to a list of do's and don'ts. People would simply rather be comfortable than uncomfortable. For example, let's say you wake up one day—you're in your 40's—and you think you've got life figured out. Really, you are just suppressed enough to survive life, there may not be any real excitement, inspiration, or fulfillment, but hey, at least you know what to predict tomorrow."

"Self-development requires discomfort. Neuroscience shows us that one of the ways in which human beings survive is by trying to predict the future—so we can be prepared and get ahead of what's coming. Our brain's job is to see a threat before it happens and respond to prevent injury, pain, or discomfort. If we are always trying to predict the future we'll create a familiar construct to live inside of to make the future that much easier to predict. Now we have comfort but it's a trade. Now there is nothing new to challenge us and nothing for us to push against, no growth is possible. The comfort is in being able to predict tomorrow so I can survive it."

"How does one get to being comfortable in unpredictability? Practice. How does someone get comfortable going to the gym on a regular basis? How is it normal for this person to have a clean car, clean email box? They practice every day."

Progress requires us to go through the awkwardness of change. In fact personal growth and development involve at least three basic steps.

Step One - Recognize Your Current State

How do you get from point A to point B if you don't know where you are? Personal growth is along a path, a continual process. Analyze where you are and be honest with yourself about where you truly are. This can be a difficult process, but a necessary one.

Step Two – Define Your Goal

You need to have clarity in your goal. Set a clear, explicit, and attainable goal.

Step Three - Planning

How do I achieve my goal? Finally, we come to our planning stage. The third step is to map out your guidelines to reach the goal. So, how do we do this? Planning!

The Warning

Be in the present. Frequently, we forget to live, accept, and enjoy the present. he quickest, easiest tool to get into the present moment is to:

1. Pause

2. Place your hand on your diaphragm (belly)

3. Breathe in and expand your diaphragm

4. Focus on long, deep breaths from the diaphragm and not shallow breaths from the chest.

This process stimulates your parasympathetic nervous system and tells our body to calm down.

Let go of the past. Holding onto poor decisions, regrets, past actions, or a th not taken can be unhealthy. One way to get released from a negative is to rite it on a piece of paper, then throw it into a fire, or the trash.

Don't borrow trouble. When I find myself anxious and worrying about things at might happen in the future, I now ask: Is this something I can control? If ere is a piece of it that I can control, I focus on the solution rather than all e things that could go wrong.

Here is a quick tool I have found helpful in the past. I picked this up at a ony Robbins "Unleash the Power Within" seminar. Tony Robbins, of course, s been a pioneer in the self-development industry.

Ask yourself three questions about what you are focusing on:

1. Am I focusing on what I have or what is missing? What we focus on expands. Keep focusing on what you have, not on what is missing. Focus on the solution, not the problem.

2. Am I focusing on what I can control or what I cannot control? When it is a situation that is completely out of your control, recognize that. You can not control it.

3. Is my focus on the past, present, or future? We want our focus to b
on the present moment. The present has the power, not the past c
future. True joy is only in the present moment.

Tune Your Gratitude

Gratitude is an emotional state that shows our recognition an
appreciation for something received. That something can be anything, actio
gesture, advice that brings us to a state of gratitude.

I view gratitude as the end process in the cycle of trauma or experiencin
disappointment. It is on the path to healing. When we can start to be gratef
for whatever experience we went through, then we are moving into a high
state. Gratitude is a practice, another skill to be honed. The more we can hon
the skill of gratitude and practice gratitude, the better off we are.

"Gratitude makes a meal a feast. It makes a house a home. It turns a little into a lot."

In our "Thrive Over Stress" corporate training, a tool that has a lot o
research behind it now, is the simple tool of gratitude. Gratitude makes a me
a feast. It makes a house a home. It turns a little into a lot.

Connoisseur of Gratitude: "... *the more you become a connoisseur of gratitud
the less you are a victim of resentment, depression, and despair. Gratitude will act
an elixir that will gradually dissolve the hard shell of your ego—your need to possess an
control—and transform you into a generous being. The sense of gratitude produces tr
spiritual alchemy, makes us magnanimous—large souled."* —Sam Kenn

Eckhart Tolle says, *"Acknowledging the good you already have in your life,
the foundation for all abundance."* There are many ways to practice gratitude.
popular gratitude exercise is keeping a gratitude journal. You write three to fiv
things every day that you are grateful for.

As we put things on paper, it makes us better thinkers because we have to structure our scattered thoughts. Writing can help us identify our feelings as well. Writing helps us to strengthen our self-discipline. If we commit to writing every day, even if it is just for 5 or 10 minutes, it builds our self-discipline muscle. That self-discipline muscle can carry over to us working out, better-ating habits, etc.

The 5-Minute Journal

Science proves the simple method of starting your day with gratitude improves your overall level of happiness. You can choose a simple, blank journal or one that provides prompts for gratitude, prioritizing, quotes, affirmations, or reflections. Leading psychology research shows those who keep a gratitude journal have higher levels of positive emotion, more joy, and feel less anxiety, loneliness, and isolation. It's simple, yet effective.

Gratitude and the Brain

In the past, I didn't understand that when my prefrontal cortex and my brain were stressed, I literally could not think. And I didn't understand the connection between my brain and my body. When we are stressed, our brain's executive function power literally can not function.

From a neurological standpoint, gratitude directly activates the brain regions associated with the neurotransmitter dopamine. We know what dopamine is, our brain feels like it's on a good drug. We practice gratitude, dopamine is released, it feels good, the "reward" neurotransmitter begins to rewire our brains to new neurotransmitter pathways. Scientific research that has been done by Emmons and McCullough, shows that those who practice gratitude, have a greater increase in determination, attention, enthusiasm, and energy compared to the other groups.

I have found the gratitude exercise below to be one of the most rewarding and therapeutic. By practicing gratitude, we connect our body with positive energy, and as a result, our brain rewards us by awakening our happy feelings (dopamine.) Many have loved practicing this rerouting or rewiring of the neurotransmitters in the brain.

To practice releasing dopamine in our brains, try the *Wheel of Focus*.

Wheel of Focus

The *Wheel of Focus* is a practice of gratitude and intention. The practice assists in releasing dopamine in our brains, which will give us that "feel good" shot and begin to rewire and reroute some of the neurotransmitters in the brain.

Remember, this is not a goal-setting practice. Oftentimes we are familiar with setting goals. When setting a goal, we are looking outside of ourselves and trying to reach something we do NOT have. With gratitude, we are appreciating what we currently have and cultivating more of it.

In the center of the circle you write what you would like to focus on. For example, cultivating more peace in your life, joy, or a healthier lifestyle. The best example that I remember was when a participant created a better relationship with her husband from this exercise! In the center of her circle she wrote, "relationship with husband." She had been married for more than 20 years. The relationship was stagnant.

In the outside circles, she began to think of all things that her husband does, like baking for her, and his profession. She later told me this exercise had a revitalizing impact on her marriage.

An example of a *Wheel of Focus* from Abraham Hicks is provided here. In the back of this book is a blank copy of a *Wheel of Focus* you may use.

Mental Balance/Reframing

Mental balance is having not only clarity but a healthy perspective. I is worth emphasizing that mental balance is not about avoiding negative thoughts; instead, it connects with positive thoughts. In one way or another we will always be exposed to adversity and problems. Developing mental balance means not allowing those negative thoughts and emotions that tip the scales too far to make us feel bad. Our goal is to solve our problems, ideally by focusing on the solutions.

Here is a cognitive tool for balance or reframing that my friend Kell Raia Light shared that I found helpful. She received this tool from **The Higdon Group**. I liked this exercise and found it helpful because I used to be overwhelmed and frustrated too often. I would say mentally or out loud several times a day, I am so overwhelmed or I am so frustrated.

When in this state, one practical tool to cognitively reframe these negative thoughts is to write down "overwhelmed" (or whatever word you are telling yourself repeatedly.) Then turn the paper over and write the opposite. That could be many things such as I am learning new ways to do things. I am in the process of creating organization and prioritizing, I am delegating and utilizing time management tools I have learned in times of busy. Then rip up the paper It's all an illusion anyway! We are responsible for our state of mind.

Check-In

One of my favorite quick tools is a simple check-in, which allows you to assess your physical, emotional, and mental state quickly. I use it in the moment when my mind is scrambling and racing as it often does. A check-in should take about 60 seconds and the steps are easy:

1. Pause and take a simple breath or two.

2. Checking in on your body's physical sensation. Is there a feeling in the pit of my stomach? How do my shoulders feel? Is my neck tight

3. Checking in on the mind. Are my thoughts racing? What am I saying

to myself? What tone am I using when I am speaking to myself? Where am I emotionally?

4. Communicate your state outward to another person.

sking for Help

I am someone who will push myself until I haven't anything left in my 1ergy tank. I have repeatedly learned the lesson of asking for help. What has hibited and stopped many others is the fear of not being capable of being a 1rden on another: "I don't want to impose or be needy."

In reality, asking for help shows strength, confidence, and resourcefulness. 1ne of the most resourceful things I did in building CROW Practice was to 1ake a list of my extended team. I intentionally not only surrounded myself ith people who could help in various situations, I knew exactly who to go to 1r what. For example, I knew who to go to for editing, for financial questions, 1r contract questions, for out-of-town points of contact, human resource sues, etc. It was incredibly valuable to have early conversations with people 1d get their agreement/buy-in before a situation even arose. For example, ngi Bellingar is an expert in recruiting so she is my go-to for filling a position 1t of town. *Asking for help doesn't make us weak, it makes us human.*

it with the Emotions

A great practical tool to let go of emotions is to feel them, sit with the notions, recognize your feelings:

- Feel them
- Experience them
- Work it through
- Use it and then . . . let it go

Self-Talk

The words we use create our world. Words have energy behind them. Rather than saying, "I am so overwhelmed," say "I'm feeling really challenged by this."

Rather than saying, "I am so stressed," say "This is a difficult experience I am going through." Rather than, "I am so busy," say "I have a lot going on right now." With a slight shift in our wording, we can reframe a challenging situation.

"With a slight shift in our wording, we can reframe a challenging situation".

Know Thyself

It is incredibly important for us to know ourselves. The concept goes back to ancient Greece. Scholars, philosophers, and others have debated this question for a long time. "Know Thyself" was carved into stone at the entrance to Apollo's temple at Delphi in Greece, according to legend. Socrates said, "To know thyself is the beginning of wisdom."

Be aware of your limitations; know what you are capable of doing. For example, I have a friend who is saddled with severe ADD (Attention Deficit Disorder). She will tell people this, to explain how she operates, and then that individual will have an understanding of her. When we know ourselves allows us to stay true to who we are and not be swayed by the environment. It also allows us to communicate effectively with others and shows compassion to ourselves.

What Does it Mean to Be an Empath?

It was later in life that I learned that I have empathic tendencies. The term empath comes from empathy, which is the ability to understand the experiences and feelings of others outside of your perspective. You sense and feel emotions as if they're part of your own experience. In other words, someone else's pain and happiness become your pain and happiness.

I believe there is a gradient scale of empaths. Empaths make up 15-20% of the population. When I was in my early 20s I didn't know the word or what it meant, or that I was an empath. I can feel what another is feeling. Many people have this gift. For those who are empaths, when we are unaware of how to balance it, it will deplete us. I, like many other empaths, am affected tremendously by my environment. Becoming a sponge or a chameleon to whatever environment we are in. It's taken most of my life to understand this balance of energy and how easily it can be depleted.

Sarah Small, the creator of The Uncensored Empath, has a quiz you can take to determine how much of an empath you are. I have listened to a number of her podcasts. I enjoyed learning about the link between autoimmune diseases and being an empath. Sarah has a lot of great resources on her site and in her podcast, her site can be found in the back of this book as well as here: https://theuncensoredempath.com/

Notes:

Chapter 3:

Tools for Busy Professionals

Carrie Abernathy CMP, CEM, CSEP: "I always think people confuse stress management and stress mitigation. We should all be trying to work on our stress mitigation so that we don't have to get to the "management" point. I think that people are VERY stressed by the time they get to the point where they are actively seeking solutions. Event professionals are consistently named in *Forbes* (and other publications) among the top five "most-stressful-jobs" each year. I also often see that Type-A planners don't give themselves any time to work on their own stress. This is a very service-forward, selfless industry. We often get to the point of exhaustion or BEYOND before we seek help. In a Yale course on well-being, I learned that there are several solutions to alleviating stress and bringing more happiness to your overall life. While there are many, I think a combination of exercise, sleep, and meditation are my top three suggestions.

Start small and work your way up. If you are at an event working until 4 am, sleep is going to be a problem, and you are probably mentally and physically exhausted. What can you do to alleviate that? Can you book yourself three minutes where you go into a dark space and listen to a brief meditation? It may seem hokey, but it truly helps calm your mind and body. Small self-care points will truly add up if you can't give yourself more time.

Busy = Success

Many people falsely equate busyness and stress with success. Why do we do this? Corporate culture will often support "busy." If a colleague asks you how you are, the appropriate response is often, "busy, busy, busy." The external activity of DOING is seen as valuable above all else.

I have lived most of my life with the environment enforcing the idea that busy = success. I value being busy. I have been attracted to industries and jobs that are incredibly fast-paced. Career jobs where the absence of sleep good diet, exercise, relaxation, and time with family and friends is the norm. thought my burnout was a badge of honor. This is changing for me.

What I am currently learning and working toward is my own state of being busy and valuing just as much as the state of peaceful awareness. An interesting challenge to think about is how does one create calm in the chao of busyness and find peace and grounding? I am on a journey with this; it is a constant balancing act for me.

A grounding technique I would suggest is simply counting. Use your fingers—the physical sensation of counting on your fingers gives your mind something to focus on, a distraction. I was almost late for a flight recently and while standing in line for security, I was becoming more and more anxious in a situation I couldn't control at that moment and regretting that I could have prevented it. Counting helped me find my calm in the chaos.

Some people tend to focus on survive rather than thrive. Even though we have the tools, we may not use them. Remember the whiteboard we discussed earlier? I love to use whiteboards. There is something about starting with a clean, blank slate and creating. It gives me a quick visual and reference of whatever I need. List your tools so you can reference them quickly.

Resenting Success

Prior to COVID, CROW Practice was getting so busy that I would often find myself working seven days a week, 10-14 hour days, just to keep up. recall having a thought, I had worked for six years to build this business and now it was reaching new heights in activity levels from years of foundation laying. I remember feeling like I had trapped myself. My quality of life was not good, I was unable to take real time off or enjoy, constant needs popping up that I had to deal with as a small business owner. I also knew I had sacrificed so much to get the business to where it was, I was prepared to sacrifice my quality of life for this "success' because I had worked so hard to get there. I did not realize that this success equaled me trapping myself in work.

I thought that what would make me happy was to build CROW Practice into something successful. I poured all of my time and energy into this fo

ars. Honestly, it was painful to realize that this "success" was not as I had
nagined.

Money Mindset

Your money mindset is how you think and feel about money. Are you of
e mindset that money comes to you easily and abundantly or that money is
ard to get and there's not a lot of it?

Maunda Land, a money coach/expert, shared her insights with me. "Most
the time people are not able to assess their mindset. They don't realize it is
tually their mindset that is limiting them. Their mindset is limiting them and
eir ability. Most people are unaware that it is due to a scarcity mentality, fear
success or fear of failure, that is limiting them and their financial growth."

"Once you do that, break those limiting beliefs, you always have to be
gnizant of where you were. It is so easy to slide back. You want to know
here you came from and where you are going in your mind, then once you
t there, stay there! It is easy to go back to your comfort zone."

"What's most important with a money mindset is being around people
ho are ahead of you in their money mindset. You can see how their mindset
orks and what they achieve. What are their habits, tools, resources? What are
ey doing that I am not? What are they investing in? Most of the time, people
ead of you are not afraid to spend money."

"I have an affirmation that says, $1,000 is like $100 to me now. Am I
eating this amount of money like it's my last? Analyze that. Do the things
at will push you; get comfortable with the uncomfortable. Push forward.
ou are regressing if you go back to that state."

"There is so much money available. Do you believe that? Do you believe
oney is hard to get? What limiting beliefs do you have? Get around those
ead of you with books, masterminds, mentorships, conferences, etc.

"The mindset that making money is hard is most likely because that is
hat you have seen. As an example, if your parents worked in a factory, you
w that. You now believe that you have to work hard to provide for your
mily."

"See something different and challenge the belief. It is not hard. I coul
do XYZ and leverage this.

"Money is a tool to be able to achieve your purpose. Your purpose :
bigger than you. If you do not have enough to fulfill your purpose, then yo
can not help others fulfill theirs. The more you have, the more you can achiev
and help others. How can you embrace having more than enough?"

An interesting correlation between income level and happiness wa
proven in a scientific paper by two psychologists/economists. They won th
Nobel Prize in economics. Danny Kahneman and Agus Deaton, showed th:
in America our emotional well-being will rise with income levels, however onc
we reach the annual salary of $75,000 our happiness levels out. The more w
earn the more we think we need. "Compared with their grandparents, today
young adults have grown up with much more affluence, slightly less happines
and much greater risk of depression and assorted social pathology," state
David Myers in the book, *The American Paradox*. Life satisfaction and incom
are correlated, but not to the level we think they are.

Strategies for Living

One quick, easy tool I learned from David Wolfe, the author o
Relationships that Work, is to ask myself the question, "Am I in survival mod
or living mode?" I can recognize survival mode if I'm worried about shor
term things. shit. Strategies for living are:

Participate fully, Give 100%, Share, Be Honest, Keep Agreements, B
Vulnerable, Risk, Trust, Be Open, Suspend Judgements, Accept, Surrende
Listen, Reflect, Be spontaneous, Be childlike.

Should - Always – Never

How we talk to ourselves can change over time based on our experienc
and learning. Anytime I use the word "should" or hear someone else us
"should," it is a warning flag for me. "Should" is often someone else's belie
system or some type of societal programming.

In a work scenario, this should be this way. I like to question why? Wh
do we do it this way? If the response is because it's the way it's always bee

done, I question if there's a better way. Does it make sense to re-address and re-examine? If it would make more sense to change a process or procedure, why can't we?

Always

"Always" and "Never" statements can create fear, obligation and guilt. The unintended effect can be to put another on the defense, to make another feel responsible or feel sorry. These statements can make someone believe their feelings are invalidated, feel unappreciated, feel disoriented, and feel guilty.

From a blog on outofthefog.website:

What NOT to Do:

If you find yourself on the receiving end of "Always" and "Never" statements:

- Don't believe everything that is said in an "Always" and "Never" statement.

- It rarely helps to get defensive and start arguing your case. This can lead directly to a Circular Conversation. When a person uses "Always" and "Never" statements, they are rarely interested in establishing objective truth. Generally, they are trying to provoke an emotional response.

- Don't reciprocate with "Always" and "Never" statements of your own.

- **What TO Do:**

- Try to see past the questionable "facts" to understand the feeling that is being communicated.

- Objectively weigh the validity of any accusations you receive when you are in a safe place with time to think.

- Share your experiences with a trusted confidant or a therapist who can help you to see the gray between the black and the white.

- Remove yourself and any children from any conversation which becomes verbally abusive or if a person refuses to stop talking after you have asked them to stop.

Rumination

If you are feeling down, it can be natural to fixate on a negative recording in your mind playing over and over. If you have low self-esteem, it can be addictive to replay the awful scenes and relive them to torture yourself.

This is not serving a healing purpose or one's higher self. This is called ruminating. Replaying what was said, what happened repeatedly. Let it go.

"For every minute you remain angry, you give up 60 seconds of peace of mind."

- Ralph Waldo Emerson

Perception

I have asked the question hundreds of times to individuals in our introduction to the "Thrive Over Stress" series. What is your most powerful stress management tool? Oftentimes people will say exercise or meditation, which are all great tools to have in our toolbox. However, according to *Psychology Today*, our most powerful stress management tool is our own perception.

Our perception has the ultimate control over each situation. The control that we have in a stressful situation is actually what gives us our ultimate power. For example, when we are in a stressful situation, we can literally lie to ourselves and convince ourselves that we have more control or power than we actually do, which will then give us the feeling that we have power and control in the situation.

The interesting thing about a stressful situation, the situation itself has little effect on your stress level and energy. It is your perception of control over stressful situations. This control can even be an illusion.

Multitasking versus Switch-Tasking

For busy people or someone who is experiencing chaos, they are force to multitask. Multitasking can even be worn as a badge of honor. Howeve studies show that multitasking increases the chances of making mistake and missing important information and cues. Multitaskers are less likely t retain information in the working memory. It can hinder problem-solving an creativity when we multitask.

So how do we juggle multiple tasks successfully? With a slight shift in ou focus and thinking from multitasking to switch tasking.

Rather than multitasking, we want to practice what is called switch-taskin Multitasking would be giving the same amount of energy to, for example, tw things, when you split your focus 50-50 or three things, dividing your focu even further. If you're doing three things simultaneously, your brain can onl give 33% of its attention to the task. The brain is being divided and being spl in several directions. When this happens, the likelihood of mistakes jump exponentially.

Switch tasking is choosing which one to focus on as the priority. Stop a much as possible doing any other tasks. You want as few pulls on your brain a possible. If you're typing on the computer and someone walks into the roon your fingers could keep going on that computer. But, if you're going to switc tasks and focus on the individual that just walked into the room, maybe it your boss, maybe it's your partner and they're asking you a direct question. Yo actually want to switch tasks, stop typing on the computer and one-hundre percent divert your attention to that question. And then switch back to th computer.

I recently spoke with Leigh Ann Krohmer, a Senior Design an Development Manager for a Destination Management Company abou multitasking:

"In all of the positions I have held I have had to multitask. I am able t jump around and complete tasks based on priority. When I really need to focu on a specific project, I like to silence my phone and turn off my email so I ca get into my creative brain, etc. I am extremely organized and that helps. Makin lists and checking things off keeps me on track. Making quick decisions abou

1at takes precedence is a skill set I have that helps with multitasking".

With priorities pulling us, jumping from project to project, call to call, :., we can lose sight of our own mental state. We are not checking in on our elings.

› find calm in the chaos, use a *Feeling Wheel*.

he Feeling Wheel

It is a visual aid that helps us recognize our feelings, talk about them, d change them. The feeling wheel has an inner core circle divided into ‹ feelings. The two outer circles are secondary feelings that relate to the ‹ primary feelings. For example, if I am feeling overwhelmed, underneath at feeling can be anxiety, and digging further in it is from a place of fear being scared. It is a tool to help build our awareness of our emotional ‹cabulary. When I am in a state of overwhelm or anxiety, I realize that what n experiencing is based on fear or being scared. There are many *Feeling Wheels* ιt there, developed by several different people. Gloria Wilcox is credited with ιe of them.

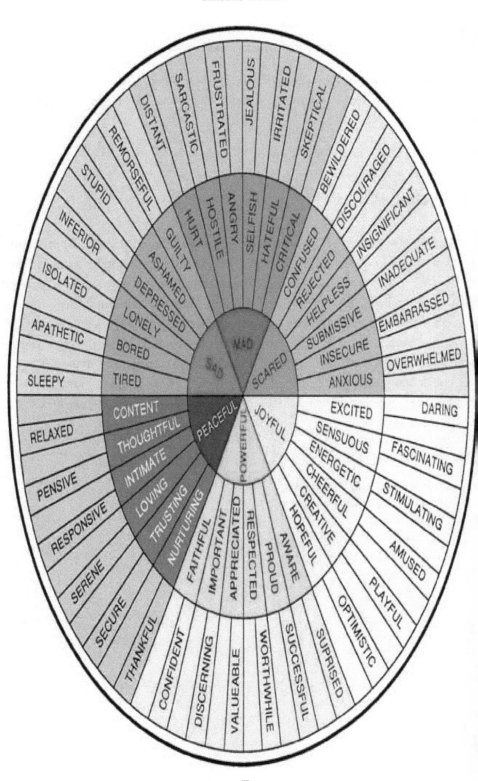

Notes:

Chapter 4

Harmony

What do we benefit from through painful experiences? Part of it is to help others. When I think of someone I know, who had an extremely painful experience yet turned "it" into something that heals, not only themself, but others, I think of my friend Rachel. A stranger broke into her home and raped her at gunpoint. She used this horrific experience to process her own pain and help other victims.

Rachel's Story

"I refer to 'it' as many things, that incident, the event, the attack. Words to describe 'it'—and purposely avoiding other words. For instance, I will avoid saying his name. I also avoid saying 'my rapist.' A lot of victims refer to their attacker as 'theirs.' I guess I don't want to put any claim on him. Because in turn that means he has a claim on me. That is not something I will allow."

"It's about taking the power back. I always say that he only had power over me during one or two hours of my life. So, I try not to let him rent space in my head any more than he deserves. I understand why victims will use 'my rapist' as a pronoun—because it's a shorter way of saying 'when I was assaulted,' 'when I was attacked,' or 'when I was raped.' Referring to 'that person' is shorter than saying 'the person that attacked me,, or 'the person that raped me.' I also have a hard time saying those words because I think that there's still a part of me in denial. They are very undeniable and commanding words, so I guess I feel if I say them out loud it will give power to that event. I don't like to give it that power."

"This was a pretty severe crime, involving a gun, carjacking, robbery, 13 felony counts. I remember the police at the time investigating it had every single man and woman they had looking for him. And I remember thinking, 'that's overkill. This stuff happens all the time. Why are they treating it like it's such a serious thing?' I think again, that was just my brain trying to minimize what it was, as some kind of survival instinct so that I could function. My brain was protecting me from going into complete shock, or ketosis."

"I think that there is always going to be a part of me that wants to deny in some way that it happened. It was so much of an enormous and life-changing thing. I will always be on a journey of healing. I don't think it is ever going to be something that stops for me. I'm just further along the road than I was when I first started. Maybe farther along than some other victims who have not received the help that they need yet or have just now been hurt. No matter what the trauma, we all start that journey in different ways. It is never the same timing or path. Sometimes it is shorter, longer, and rockier."

"I was very lucky to have been taken to the Victim Service Center. I started receiving treatment and counseling immediately, within 24 hours. A lot of people aren't that lucky. A lot of people also don't have the support system that I had. I had an incredibly large and strong group of women in my life that came to my aid in ways I didn't even know I needed at the time. I had a strong family foundation that was there for me. Not a lot of victims can say that. Or worse, and a lot more common, it is someone from that very same support system that hurt them. I was also lucky enough to have been believed. Everybody that came across my story, from a friend, to cops, and family, they never questioned me. Whether that's because I'm a white woman who was raped by a black man, I don't know. It is entirely possible that my privilege allowed me that support, which is something I have thought about while helping other victims. It's unfortunate, yes, but I can't change that. It is just how society reacted to my event. More than anything else, I try to focus on the positive things that can come out of all of it."

"I direct a lot of my energy in community outreach and volunteering and speaking whenever I can, to share my story. I feel that if there's *just one* thing that someone can get from my story, that either helps them or can help somebody else, then that makes what happened to me more worth it. It goes back to the power of the event, and the more I can turn that into a positive thing, the less it is a negative. *I* choose how the energy is shifted and in what direction, which ultimately puts the power back in my hands. Like anything in life, it is a balance. There's a good and bad side of everything. It all comes down to what you choose to focus on. I try to focus on the positive things, my friends, family, husband, my daughter—rather than 1 1/2 hours in my life and how I decide to live the rest of it."

Decide to Take Your Power Back

You have the ultimate choice: you have decision-making responsibility to navigate your life by your thoughts and words. There is a tool, a method, a way to accept something quicker so you can move on. Sometimes when life hands you lemons, we don't automatically make lemonade. However, a tool and a practice to help ourselves move on is to *decide*. Decide that you have the control and the power in the situation. You get furloughed from your job. Are you going to wait on that company? Are you going to wait on that job? How can you take the power back? Don't let someone else decide your direction for you because you are the captain of your own ship.

Getting Unstuck (Emotionally)

My friend Allison Carmeny, a spiritual intuitive, helped me identify that I have a pattern that has been stuck since childhood, as a "victim." Instead of me knowing that I am, and get to be, the creator of my reality. I fell prey to the outside world impacting me. Instead of knowing that everything is working for me. I felt the world at times was working against me. As a result of this

Kristine Iverson

shift in perspective, it has allowed me to take full responsibility and contro of my life. To become the creator of my story and the world I want to crea within me and around me.

Allison also introduced me to another tool to move through negativ emotions quickly, Ho'oponopono. The Hawaiian word Ho'oponopono com from ho'o ("to make") and pono ("right"). The repetition of the word pon means "doubly right" or being right with both self and others. In a nutshe Ho'oponopono is a process by which we can forgive others to whom w are connected. Ho'oponopono is a traditional Hawaiian prayer and it's sup simple. Say this to yourself:

1. Say "I'm sorry"

2. Please forgive me

3. Thank you

4. I love you

These four steps of Ho'oponopono represent repentance, forgivenes gratitude, and love. This practice of forgiveness is a communication tool well as a tool for restoring our own self-love and balance.

Getting Unstuck (Mentally)

Mel Robbins is a personal favorite of mine, as someone to watch follow/listen to. During COVID she would go live daily and simply be re with people. She shared action steps to getting unstuck.

Tool to get "unstuck" - Mel Robbins - Action Steps

1. Download – Create lists, brain dump on a white-board, tasks, an timing

2. Divide - Break it down into small chunks - Use post-it notes i necessary

3. Do it - It will not get done all at once - Can you delegate anything?

Self-Compassion

"Developing self-compassion is critical. I wish I could go back in time and tell the younger me that I needed to focus on self-compassion."

Developing self-compassion is critical. I wish I could go back in time and tell the younger me that I needed to focus on self-compassion. When I started something new I would stop because of negative self-talk. I had not built the muscle of speaking kindly to myself.

The journey of self-compassion is a lifetime journey. It's a part of our well-being journey. If and when I ever get off the path of my own self-compassion I am now aware that it is critical to jump back on the path. It's worth it to invest time, energy, and resources in learning how to do that.

For Lisa Jennings, Chief Experience Officer for Wildly Different, if she could give her younger self a message she would say, "Don't worry too much about what people think of you. We are all on a different path in life—no one path is right. Just go out and live the life that makes YOU and the people you care about happy and the rest will fall in place".

Kristin Neff in her TED Talk speaks about how in American culture we have high self-esteem and we need to feel special and above average. This contributes to an epidemic of narcissism in our country, possibly due to the self-esteem movement in schools. If we all have to feel above average to gain self-esteem, then we are comparing ourselves and making ourselves better by putting others down.

Self-compassion is not about judging ourselves positively. It is about relating to ourselves *kindly*. There are three core components to treating oneself with kindness.

First, how do we treat ourselves on a bad day? Like we would a good friend or are we cruel to ourselves? We oftentimes can be our own worst enemy. When you practice loving-kindness towards a loved one, someone you truly care about like a child or parent, then you extend this kindness to yourself, a neutral person, an enemy, and then all beings. It is fascinating to experience how easy it is to send loving kindness to someone you truly adore. Then it can be different towards oneself and often challenging and possibly healing to send loving kindness to someone you consider an enemy.

The second component is common humanity. Self-esteem asks how am I different from others? Self-compassion asks how am I the same? To be human means to be imperfect. The shared human experience.

The third component is mindfulness. Being with what is in the present moment. Accept the suffering to give ourselves compassion. At times we are unaware we are suffering.

Why are we cruel to ourselves? We believe we need our self-criticism to motivate ourselves. If we do not, then we will be lazy. Is it true? No research shows the opposite. When we self-criticize, we are tapping into our reptile brain. Attacker and the attacked. This leads to stress. Fight or flight response, the threat is not to our physical body, to our self-concept. Attack the problem—self. When we have high self-criticism, we release cortisol. The body will protect itself and shut down.

When we practice self-compassion we are bringing ourselves to the optimum mindset for our best. Our bodies release the feel-good drugs oxytocin and dopamine. Our bodies' natural feel-good release is strongly related to our mental well-being, happiness, self-responsibility, and healthier lifestyle choices. Associated with strong mental health benefits of self-esteem without the pitfalls. Not associated with narcissism, comparing, unstable sense of self-worth. When self-esteem deserts you, self-compassion steps in and it kindly connects you back to humanity.

If we are being cruel to ourselves, we can reverse this with self-compassion. Zen Buddhist monk, Thich Nhat Hahn, has a great self-compassion meditation. Give it a try here: https://www.youtube.com/watch?v=q56_jZagIJ0.

And when I think back to my ship experience and how I was talking to myself, when I look at my old journals from the ship and directly afterward there was very little to no self-love that I had for myself. I was not being compassionate to myself. If anything, I was tearing myself down. I was incredibly critical of myself and others. I had not learned compassion for myself or self-love.

Calm in the Chaos

We truly are responsible for our thoughts. We are responsible for our actions to ourselves and others because ultimately if COVID has taught us anything, it's that we are all connected at an unseen level and in ways to the extent and capacity that many of us do not realize on a daily basis. I am adamant that a moment in time would never define me or my future. It doesn't. One moment does not define me and I've practiced these tools to create calm in the chaos.

I created a wellness company focused on bringing self-care and healing modalities to busy professionals. I believe that my strong desire to do this stems from my first ship experience. Only in retrospect can I look back and make the connection. This terrifying experience that I did not share with people, ruled my decision-making for years in the background.

Yogic Path

I tried yoga a few times in my early 20s. I didn't fully connect with it enough to keep exploring. My understanding of yoga was a physical component and yet I understood there was something much greater in the essence of yoga. However, I was blocked and stopped myself from exploring yoga. In retrospect, I can see several gentle, supportive friends who were encouraging me to explore yoga. I just didn't get into it. I tried a few classes and wasn't committed to further exploring the path of yoga. I recall I wanted more of a physical workout. If I was carving out an hour a day to work out, it made more logical sense to get my cardio in, right?

A dear friend told me that yoga would be really good for me. I was given a yoga mat for Christmas one year. I had extreme anxiety in general and chose not to pursue yoga at that point in life. I wonder what my life would look like if I had followed yoga then . . .

Yoga - Connection to Self

I was in between cruise ship contracts and had all the time in the world for yoga. I practiced yoga every single day for two weeks. That is the first time that I noticed subtle changes, not simply in my body physically, it was *energetic* changes. For example, in life off the mat, a decision needed to be made: choose A or choose B. I energetically or intuitively knew that choosing B was going to be a higher, better pathway. My body would tell me and I could feel the best path, decision to be made. I didn't have to debate in my mind, didn't have to second guess myself. I simply knew the answer, I could FEEL it in my body! I knew that I wanted a yoga practice to become part of my life. When I completed my career on ships, I signed up for yoga training at Firefly Yoga Company in Orlando, with Holly Garrison.

Holly has a gift for creating community. She genuinely cares for each soul that walks through her doors at Firefly. She is someone who embodies yoga off the mat and in her daily life. For anyone who has studied the philosophy of yoga, the practice of yoga goes well beyond the physical asanas or postures. This poem was shared in our yoga training, I left like it encompassed a beautiful description of yoga, beyond the poses themselves.

The State of Yoga by Candice Martin

The state of yoga is not solely found in a posture. It requires little more than one's ability to rest in the beauty of exactly who they are. The state of yoga flourishes in the arms of self-acceptance and unfolds as endless guidance through self-trust. In other words, yoga occurs when we are fully ourselves. The tools, limbs, petals of this ancient system help us arrive there. And once this elusive state is mustered through practice, everyone benefits. An entire community thrives. Yoga begins to show up as a magnet of a nourishing restaurant offering love and wellness. Or a studio that flings its doors wide open without judgment, with complete wholeness, embracing all. Yoga arrives in classrooms, it shows up in the love for our children and the children of others. Yoga is the parent who relentlessly works to bring these tools to our schools. It's dance, it's art, it's theater, it's study, and surrender. It is the brave knowledge that through our vulnerability, humanity, and humility, we have already arrived.

Follow the Body Language

After having visited more than 40 countries, thanks to my experienc with international cruise lines, I saw what science and research confirm: th body language carries more meaning than words. It is much more univers than spoken or written language. The more you learn to read expressions, tl better you communicate with others.

One of my favorite talks about body language is Amy Cuddy's TED Tal "Your Body Language May Shape Who You Are." She references the pow pose and explains if you stand in a Wonder Woman pose, hands on hip chest out, shoulders back, your testosterone increases (in women, too), cortis decreases, you become more risk-taking. Studies have found that people pain threshold becomes higher and they are more likely to do well in stressf situations using the right body language.

Raise Your Vibration

When the live events industry shifted to virtual, one of our best sellers w offering 15-minute breaks for the meeting marathons. A popular request was for a energy booster session. The reasons for low energy can vary. When in a mental fc the best energy pick-me-up is to move! Our bodies are meant to move, not sit in chair for eight hours a day. Taking more, shorter breaks throughout the day may see counterintuitive, but it actually boosts productivity and efficiency.

A quick breath technique that is shared frequently in the yoga community raise our energy levels and purify our blood is the breath of fire. It is done with long inhale with many short forceful exhales from your abdomen. The exhale, whic requires you to contract your abdominal muscles, is the main focus of this techniqu While pumping the navel you are breathing rapidly through your nose with the mou closed. I will add a caution here because the breath of fire has been compared how you breathe when hyperventilating. I do want to make a distinction between tl two in case you ever feel like you are going to pass out while doing the breath of fir STOP. It is meant to be quick-paced and sustained for a long period of time. Yc never want to pass out or hyperventilate.

Emotional Scale

It is proven that everything is energy, including even our thoughts and emotions. Even our emotions have a frequency or vibration. Energy and emotions vibrate at a certain frequency just as sound does.

The below scale shows different emotions and where they are on the emotional scale. Lowest on the scale is fear, greif, despair and powerlessness. The emotional energy of the lower states are heavy and can pull you down. You want to focus on the higher emotional energy states, which can feel fluid, move towards joy and appreciation.

Joy/Appreciation/Empowered/Freedom/Love

Passion

Enthusiasm/Eagerness/Happiness

Positive Expectation/Belief/Optimism

Hopefulness

Contentment

Boredom

Pessimism

Frustration/Irritation/Impatience

Overwhelment

Disappointment

Doubt

Worry

Blame

Discouragement

Anger/Revenge

Hatred/Rage

Jealousy

Insecurity/Guilt/Unworthiness

Fear/Grief/Despair/Powerlessness

Move UP the emotional scale

Debugging - Worst Case Scenario

Worst Case Scenario is another tool to help us realign our thoughts when we are in a negative loop. If we think of our brains as a computer, just as computers can get a bug, our brains can get a bug. We have to debug ourselves continually. How? Through a check-in process, journaling, and/or asking ourselves what are our beliefs?

We want to identify our own thought processes and patterns. Ultimately our underlying beliefs create our thought processes and take us in a direction. We want to be aware and conscious of where our beliefs are so that when we have an incorrect, limiting belief, we can recognize it and ask ourselves what is the Worse Case Scenario in this situation?

Anytime you are in a stressful situation, or when you have to make a difficult choice, you ask yourself, what is the worst-case scenario? And play it out. So, for example, let's say you lose your job. In reality, you can't change that situation. You've lost your job. What is the worst-case scenario that can actually happen here? The worst-case scenario is you can't pay your bills and you're not going to be able to buy food and/or you're going to be evicted from your home. How much truth is there in that? Are there other means to go about the scenario? How far can savings and credit cards get you?

Follow the fear all the way through and if that is honestly a real possibility, follow it through to the end. Maybe you don't have to be homeless on the streets and hungry. Maybe if you lost your home, you have a friend or family member you could stay with? Would you fall back on a support system? Some of our fears are not even real. Granted losing one's job can be extremely stressful. You will have to re-adjust and often quickly. So the worst-case scenario is honestly not that you'll be homeless on the streets, more that you will deplete savings and possibly worse case, couch surf.

Dharma & Purpose

Dharma literally means "right way of living" or "path of rightness," with the implication that there is a right or true way for each person to live their life in order to serve both themselves and others.

The meaning of the word dharma depends on the context, and its meaning has evolved as ideas of Hinduism have developed through history.

[Please note: this definition differs from Buddhist thought where dharma can mean doctrine or the universal truth common to all people at all times, specifically proclaimed by the Buddha. Dharma is one of the Three Jewels of Buddhism.]

In life, there are books you find at the right time. I was in constant search of my purpose, what do I do with my life? Then I read, *The Great Work of Your Life: A Guide for the Journey to Your True Calling*, by Stephen Cope, and I found the clarity that I had been searching for years for.

In his book, Cope says that to have a fulfilling life you must discover the deep purpose hidden at the very core of yourself. The secret to unlocking this mystery, he asserts, can be found in the pages of a thousands-year-old spiritual classic called the *Bhagavad Gita*. *Bhagavad Gita* is an ancient allegory about the path to dharma, told through a timeless dialogue between the fabled archer, Arjuna, and his divine mentor, Krishna. If you're feeling lost in your own life's journey, I highly recommend *The Great Work of Your Life*—it truly helped me find my path.

My Path

I gained more clarity around a sense of my true purpose when I was going through my yoga certification. I was on the fence about getting certified. Now I am so grateful I did. I understand my dharma because I am fully choosing If we are the navigators and masters of our lives, then being able to bring holistic healing modalities into the corporate realm is my purpose, my dharma.

Many are searching for meaning, as I did for years. How does one find that they are meant to do? How do we discern our dharma? I will occasionally just out my notes on Cope's book:

1. Trust in your gifts

2. Think of the small as large

3. Listen for the call of the time

The gift in my life at the time was yoga, a practice that was leading me back to myself."

I began to *trust in my gifts*. The gift in my life at the time was yoga, a practice that was leading me back to myself. I began trusting in myself more. Thinking of the small as large.

In the first year of building CROW Practice, *the small was large*. We had a handful of corporate clients. From a business standpoint, it was small. To me, it was large and so important.

The *call of the time* in my heart was simply to share healing with others. I wanted to do it on a larger scale. I had experience in the meetings and events industry, however, I was not even targeting them nor had I created a clear plan strategy yet.

Transform Purpose Into Creative Action

I love stepping back and taking the time to create yearly, quarterl
monthly goals, all while knowing that there are going to be adjustments. Ou
vision, desires, and goals for what we want shift and change. Roadblocks po
up. The life I'm intentionally creating for myself in my 40s is vastly differer
from the life I was intentionally creating for myself in my 20s.

I am fortunate to surround myself with artists. I believe our creativ
expression can literally save lives. It can help us tap into deep dark emotion
process and release. My friend Nicole Depre, lost her ex-husband to an opio
addiction. She then created Opera del Sol and a breathtaking Fringe sho
addressing addiction and death. This was a process for her that allowed h
to heal. I enjoy looking for activities that inspire more creative living activitie
For me, that's thrift store shopping, workshops, seminars, improv classes, c
being in nature. Take the time to find your creative outlets and what inspir
you.

Receive the Magic

You are most likely familiar with Maslow's "Hierarchy of Needs." It
a pyramid where the bottom is survival and we cannot move up the pyram
without our basics covered first. Survival is basic. When I find myself in th
state of survival, I remind myself to have compassion with where I AM. In th
first year that I started CROW Practice, I was renting a room from a homeown
and the situation became toxic. The homeowner became aggressive and I ha
to get out. I posted something on Facebook and something magical happene
A woman who I did not know (or even had any mutual friends with) offere
to let me stay in her million-dollar home downtown while she traveled! Ye
Then in our phone conversation, she mentioned that she had two dogs. I sa
I would take care of them while she traveled. She then said I could stay in h
million-dollar mansion home only in exchange for watching her dogs! I wa
so blown away and taken back by this amazing generosity, that I refused th
offer!! It was an amazing gift that I was not in a state to accept! When I realize
what I had done, I called her back and said yes! "Yes, I will watch your pups
exchange for rent." (I would have watched the pup's just because, who doesr
love dogs?!)

Manifestation Box

Manifestation Box is a fun creation tool to use if you are in the process of doing something that you have concerns or reservations about. For example, you are going to speak publicly and you're nervous or in your own head about it. You can pull out a box, paper, colored pens.

Start by writing positive outcomes that you envision on each piece of paper, then put them in the box. You can write things like, "I see myself being confident." "Feedback was positive from attendees." "The question-and-answer period was brilliant." "We got great marketing photos and it was a success."

You are manifesting or envisioning the success of your project ahead of time. After the event, pull the pieces of paper out of the box and see which ones you manifested or created.

Clarity Tool

Another creation tool that I love is simply asking yourself four questions. These bring clarity to you as well as the universe:

1. What do I want today?

2. What does it look like?

3. How does it feel in my body?

4. What do I tell myself?

These four questions are a great way to start a day, a project, or experience. The clearer we are with what we want to create, the better the universe can, does, and will respond. When we are unclear, the universe cannot work in that unclarity.

Fresh Perspective

Kids bring a fresh, fun perspective to life. In the summer of 2021, I wa able to spend a week with my 12-year niece, Annabelle, who lives far awa from me. And I learned that she is an impressive kid! I was reminded that wha eighth-graders struggled with in middle school is not all that different fron what some adults are struggling with. The kids haven't had the life experienc that adults have, but they have similar struggles.

I loved learning more about anime, Minecraft, YouTube stars, and new musical artists. I'm excited about all the opportunities she has before her. Sh can literally do anything—the world is open with so many possibilities for he

This was the first time we'd had so much one-on-one time and Annabell brought an unexpected, fresh perspective to my life. So often we do the same old, same old and don't even realize we are stuck in a rut. Finding a fresh, new perspective can release a new creative outlet and can turn the mundane int new and exciting. I highly recommend you try new things to find your fresh perspective.

Final Thoughts

I am grateful to my friends who were honest with me and told me tha you have a lot of depth as a person and I don't see much of that here. *Calm in the Chaos*,has been an exciting first time journey of writing and publishin a book, it was a huge personal goal. It took a lot of self-drive to accomplish Calm in the Chaos has allowed me to become an advocate for mental healtl and wellness, speaking on the topic openly. I envision a world where we ca speak about mental health honestly and openly. These important conversation should not be taboo, with no difference between a healthy conversation abou our nutrition plan. I believe normalizing mental health discussions woul reveal our humanity and remind us that self-care is essential. I want to be a par of breaking the stigma around mental health and invite you to do the same.

Covid has challenged us all when it comes to mental health. At on point there was hope for us to go back to normal. However, as the pandemi continues, we've realized this is our reality and the precautions we once though to be temporary, are most likely our new normal. Since we experienced this collective trauma, many are speaking about their own mental health more openly. Be Well TV has a weekly check in of where hosts ask how are you this week? It's an honest deep dive from those in the events industry, speaking openly and honestly about their mental state in addition to other aspects of health. Be Well TV can be found on youtube. (Link in e-book)

My hope is that you find at least one helpful tool or resource in Calm in the Chaos. If you do, then I will consider it a success.

Blank Wheel of Focus:

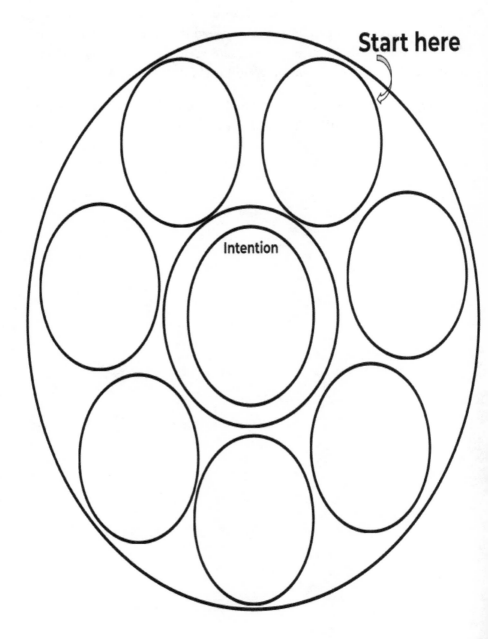

Start here

Intention

Notes:

References & Notes

Lyubomirsky (2007). **The How of Happiness: A New Approac** **to Getting the Life You Want.** New York, NY: Penguin Books.

Csikszentmihalyi, M. (1990). **Flow: The Psychology of Optim:** **Experience.** New York: Harper & Row.

Martin Seligman (2011) **Flourish: A New Understanding (** **Happiness and Well-Being - and how to Achieve Them.** Nichol: Brealey Publishing.

David Myers (2000) **The American Paradox: Spiritual Hung** **in an Age of Plenty.** Yale University Press publications.

Stephen Cope (2012) **The Great Work of Your Life: A Guid** **for the Journey to Your True Calling.** Penguin Random House.

David Wolfe - (2017) **Relationships that work. The Power (** **Conscious living.** BabyBook.com

Paul Hammerness MD (Author), Margaret Moore (Author (2011) Organize Your Mind, Organize Your Life. Harlequin Publishir

Emmons and McCullough (2003) Positive Psychology Practice. John Wiley & Sons, Inc.

Websites:

As of August 3, 2021, The uncensored empath listed on i website:

https://theuncensoredempath.com/

As of August 3, 2021, the Psychcentral.com listed on its websit

https://psychcentral.com/lib/10-way-to-build-and-preserve better-boundaries#the-lowdown

As of August 3, 2021the website: https://thebrain.mcgill.ca/

As of August 3, 2021 the website:

https://www.simpleserenity.com/mindful-minutes/connoisseur-of-gratitude/

As of August 9th, 2021 the website:

The Hertz Scale - https://spacioustherapy.com/understanding-emotions/

As of August 3, 2021 the website:

https://markmanson.net/limiting-beliefs

As of August 3, 2021 The uncensored empath listed on it's website:

https://theuncensoredempath.com/

Kristin Neff, The Space Between Self Esteem and Self Compassion, TED, Feb. 6, 2013, https://www.youtube.com/watch?v=IvtZBUSplr4

Amy Cuddy, Your Body Language May Shape Who You Are, TED, Oct. 1, 2012,

https://www.youtube.com/watch?v=Ks-_Mh1QhMc&t=232s

Gloria Willcox (1982) The Feeling Wheel

https://allthefeelz.app/feeling-wheel/

https://spacioustherapy.com/understanding-emotions/

Thich Nat Hahn has a great self-compassion meditation. Give it a try here: https://www.youtube.com/watch?v=q56_jZagIJ0

PERMA quiz - citation to the article (Butler & Kern, 2016) - https://www.peggykern.org/uploads/5/6/6/7/56678211/the_perma-profiler_101416.pdf

Be Well TV-??

Conclusion & Invitation

I am practicing being okay with "imperfect" and "letting go" with m book journey. I will be happy to receive constructive criticism to improve thi text and to grow as a person. I sincerely welcome any and all suggestions fo improvement.

If you liked this book, I kindly ask you to leave a review on the Amazor page dedicated to this book. If you would like to reach out to discuss how w can normalize mental health, I'd love to hear from you.

If you are not satisfied or you have suggestions to make, I can b contacted directly:

www.KristineIverson.com

www.CROWPractice.com

calminthechaos@gmail.com

Resources-Mental Health, Self-Care, Holistic Doctor, Coaches, etc.

National Institute for Mental Health

Information, Resources & Inquiries Branch

5600 Fishers Lane

Rockville, MD 20857

301-443-4513

800-421-4211

nimhpub@nih.gov

Dr. Marni F. Stahlman

President/CEO

The Mental Health Association of Central Florida

https://www.mhacf.org/

Mental Health Resource: https://www.rethink.org/get-involved/awareness-days-and-events/time-to-talk-day/

VSC:

https://www.victimservicecenter.org/

Yvette Sechrist McGlasson

Wholistic Wellness Coach

Escapehatch2wellness.com

You could purchase one or create your own?

Amazon - The 5-Minute Journal

Carrie Abernathy CMP, CEM, CSEP

CEO, A Woman With Drive www.awomanwithdrive.com

CPSIA information can be obtained
at www.ICGtesting.com
Printed in the USA
BVHW081357261021
619919BV00002B/112